TREE LIFE

TREE LIFE

PHOTOGRAPHED BY
KIM TAYLOR

WRITTEN BY
THERESA GREENAWAY

DK

DK PUBLISHING, INC.

DK

A DK PUBLISHING BOOK

Senior editor Christiane Gunzi **Senior art editor** Val Wright
Editor Sue Copsey **Art editor** Julie Staniland
Design assistant Lucy Bennett
Production Louise Barratt
Illustrations Nick Hall
Index Jane Parker
Managing editor Sophie Mitchell
Managing art editor Miranda Kennedy
U.S. editor B. Alison Weir

Consultants
Barry Clarke, Andy Currant,
Paul Hillyard, Tim Parmenter, Edward Wade

With thanks to Sarah Anderson of London Zoo, Jane Burton, the London Butterfly House, Surrey
Water Gardens, and Kim Taylor for supplying some of the animals photographed in this book.
Asian tree frog, p.16, photographed by Frank Greenaway

First American Edition, 1992
First Paperback Edition, 1998
4 6 8 10 9 7 5 3

Published in the United States by
DK Publishing, Inc., 95 Madison Avenue, New York, New York, 10016.
Visit us on the World Wide Web at http://www.dk.com

Library of Congress Cataloging-in-Publication Data
Taylor, Kim.
Tree Life/photographed by Kim Taylor; written by Theresa Greenaway
p. cm. – (Look closer)
Includes index.
Summary: Describes various animals that live on or in trees, including
the butterfly, woodpecker, and tree frog.
ISBN 0-7894-3477-6
1. Natural history–Juvenile literature. 2. Habitat (Ecology)–Juvenile literature.
3. Plants–Habitat–Juvenile literature. 4. Forest fauna–Juvenile literature.
[1. Forest animals.]
1. Greenaway, Theresa, 1947- II. Title. III. Series.
QH48.T33 1992
591.52'642–dc20
92-52824–CIP–AC

Colour reproduction by Colourscan, Singapore
Printed and bound in China by L.Rex Printing Co., Ltd.

CONTENTS

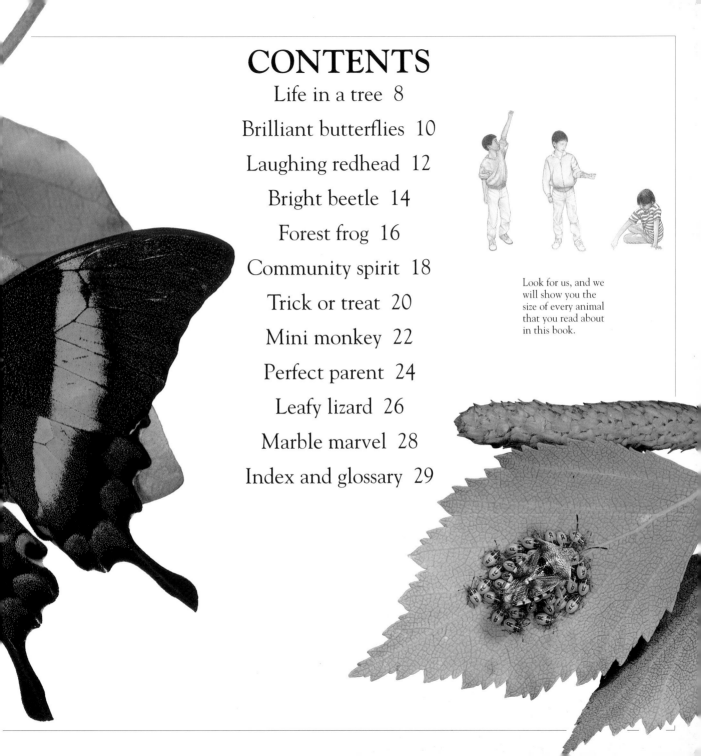

Look for us, and we will show you the size of every animal that you read about in this book.

LIFE IN A TREE

WHETHER A TREE LIVES in the warm tropics or somewhere cool, it is not just a large plant with a huge, woody trunk and a crown of leaves. A tree is a complete life support system for all sorts of different animals. Some, such as wood ants, are visitors. For them, a tree is a pantry, full of insect food. Other animals live among its branches, either eating insects, or the leaves, flowers, and fruits of the tree itself. Even more creatures make their homes inside the tree, in tree holes or beneath the bark. Gall wasp larvae (grubs) live in special round structures, called galls, that the tree makes for them. Woodlands all over the world are being chopped down for their timber, and to clear space for farming and housing. But when a forest is cut down, it is not just the trees that are lost. All the tree-life disappears, too

The marble gall wasp (*Andricus kollari*) is 5 mm long and lives in Asia, Europe, and North Africa.

The Madagascar day gecko (*Phelsuma madagascariensis*) is 6 1/2 in. long and lives in East Africa and Indian Ocean islands.

The puss moth caterpillar (*Cerura vinula*) is 2 1/2 in. long and lives in Asia, Europe, and North Africa.

The chalcid wasp (*Torymus nitens*) is 5 mm long and lives in Europe.

The Asian tree frog (*Polypedates dennysi*) is 4 1/2 in. long and lives in Southeast Asia.

The green woodpecker (*Picus viridis*) is 13 in. long and lives in Europe, Iran, Pakistan, and Turkey.

The cardinal beetle *(Pyrochroa coccinea)* is 3/4 in. long and lives in Europe.

The common marmoset's *(Callithrix jacchus)* body is 9 in. long, and it lives in Brazil.

The parent bug *(Elasmucha grisea)* is 1/2 in. long and lives in Asia and Europe.

The swallowtail butterfly *(Papilio palinurus)* has a wingspan of 4 in. and lives in Southeast Asia.

The wood ant *(Formica rufa)* is 1/4 in. long and lives north of the Equator.

BRILLIANT BUTTERFLIES

THESE BEAUTIFUL swallowtail butterflies flash in the sunlight as they fly among the trees of the tropical rain forest. The male jealously guards his territory (the area where he lives), chasing other males away. The female lays her eggs on the underside of a leaf. When the caterpillars hatch out, they are a brownish color. As they grow, they molt (shed their skin) several times. Each time they molt, they become greener, until they are bright green. When the caterpillar is fully grown, it turns into a pupa. Its skin becomes hard, like a shell, and it does not move or eat for about two weeks. During this time many changes take place, until eventually the shell splits and a colorful butterfly emerges. This transformation is called metamorphosis.

SUGAR SUCKER
The swallowtail butterfly feeds on nectar. This is the sweet, sugary liquid produced by flowers. It uses its long, tubelike mouthpart, called a proboscis, to suck up the nectar, in the same way that you use a straw to suck up a drink.

The eyespots confuse predators, which mistake them for the butterfly's head.

When the proboscis is not being used to suck nectar, it is neatly coiled under the head.

The legs are long enough to hold the body clear of objects that might get in its way.

NOW YOU SEE IT, NOW YOU DON'T
The bright colors on the upper surface of the wings are easily seen by enemies such as birds. So as soon as it lands, the swallowtail folds its wings together. The undersides of the wings are brown, so the butterfly blends in with the forest background, making it difficult to see.

These brownish colors help the swallowtail blend in with its surroundings.

The abdomen contains the organs for reproduction and for digesting food.

FALSE EYES
The orange areas on the wings are called eyespots. They help protect the swallowtail by confusing its enemies, such as birds. They peck at an eyespot, mistaking it for the butterfly's head. So only the wings are damaged.

The butterfly uses its front legs for cleaning these antennae.

The antennae (feelers) detect smells. They also help the butterfly balance.

The large compound eyes are made up of lots of individual lenses.

PARKING IN PUDDLES
Male swallowtail butterflies spend most of their time high up among the trees, but occasionally they come down to drink in puddles and damp patches on the forest floor. It is not just the moisture that attracts them. They also need salt from the soil, which is dissolved in the water.

This network of hollow tubes, called veins, strengthens the insect's wings.

These wings are large and strong so the butterfly can fly quickly.

GUESS WHAT?
This butterfly is named after a bird. The long, forked shape of its back wings is much like the shape of a swallow's tail, hence the name "swallowtail."

LAUGHING REDHEAD

THE GREEN WOODPECKER'S loud, laughing call is unmistakable. You will often hear this bird long before you can see it. When it appears, in a flash of green, red, and yellow, the green woodpecker is instantly recognizable. It spends much of its time in among the trees, especially those on the edge of meadows and parks. It also comes down to the ground to look for insects, berries, and seeds to eat. The green woodpecker spends most of its life on its own. In spring, however, it pairs up with a mate. It builds its nest in a hole in a tree, and usually lays between five and seven eggs. Both parents incubate the eggs (keep them warm), and look after the young, called nestlings, once they have hatched.

CLEVER CLIMBER
The green woodpecker climbs up a tree trunk in jerky hops. Each foot has four toes ending in sharp, powerful claws. These help the woodpecker get a firm grip on the bark. Holding on tightly with its feet, the bird balances itself with its short, stiff tail.

TREE HOUSE
When it is time to build a nest, the green woodpecker chooses a tree where it can chip the wood away easily, such as a decaying oak or pine tree. The male and female take turns hammering away at the wood. The entrance to the nest hole is usually only about 3 in. wide, but inside it is much wider and about 12 in. deep, so there is plenty of room.

The tail is short and is made of stiff feathers which support the woodpecker as it climbs.

These bright green beech leaves have just unfurled from their protective cases.

NO HEADACHES

When the woodpecker hammers at wood with its beak, strong vibrations (movements) pass up the beak and into the head. To absorb these vibrations and protect the brain, there is a special layer between the bones of the beak and the rest of the head bones. This layer is made of a flexible, rubbery substance, called cartilage. For added protection, the front part of the skull is extra hard.

These flight feathers are strong and stiff. They help the woodpecker change direction as it flies.

STICKY LICKER

The green woodpecker has an incredibly long tongue that can stick out of its beak by as much as 2 in. The tip of the tongue is covered with lots of sticky saliva. When the woodpecker pokes its tongue into an ant's nest, or into holes in rotten wood, any insects inside get stuck fast.

The tip of the tongue is covered with sticky saliva for catching insects.

This long, narrow tongue easily picks out insects from cracks in the bark.

The beak is straight and strong for chipping wood.

The sharp eyes keep a lookout for food and danger.

Both male and female green woodpeckers have a scarlet cap on their heads.

Red feathers like a moustache show that this bird is a male. Females have a black "moustache."

The bird holds its legs and feet close to its body during flight.

GUESS WHAT?

These birds are called woodpeckers because they use their strong, sharp beaks for boring into wood. They do this to chip out a nesting hole or catch insects for food.

The neck is very strong, so that it can support the head as the woodpecker hammers holes in wood.

BRIGHT BEETLE

THE BRILLIANTLY colored back of a cardinal
beetle makes it easy to recognize. These beetles look
like tiny red helicopters as they fly around
in spring and early summer, feeding
on the pollen of flowers. Female
cardinal beetles lay their eggs in
cracks in the bark of trees or logs.
They choose unhealthy trees, because
the eggs hatch into larvae (grubs) that feed on
rotting wood and fungus just beneath the bark. This
kind of food is not very nourishing, so it may take a year
or more before each larva is ready to pupate (go into a
resting stage). The beetles that hatch from each pupa
only live for about one month. During this time, they
must find and mate with another beetle. To make this
easier, cardinal beetles all hatch at about the same time.

The antennae
(feelers) are
sensitive to touch.
They are also good
at detecting smells,
even very faint ones.

The wings, the wing
cases, and the six
legs are all
attached to the
thorax (the middle
part of the body).

Each wing is
made of a thin,
transparent
(clear) skin,
called a
membrane.

A tough
exoskeleton
protects the
fragile body.

Hooks at the ends
of the legs help the
beetle climb up
trees and cling on to
leaves and flowers.

AERODYNAMICS
Cardinal beetles fly through the air
quite slowly, using their thin,
transparent wings. The wings have no
muscles inside. Instead, they are
supported by stiff veins, which
strengthen them. Special muscles
inside the thorax move each wing up
and down. When the beetle is not
flying, the wings are folded away
tightly under the elytra (wing cases).

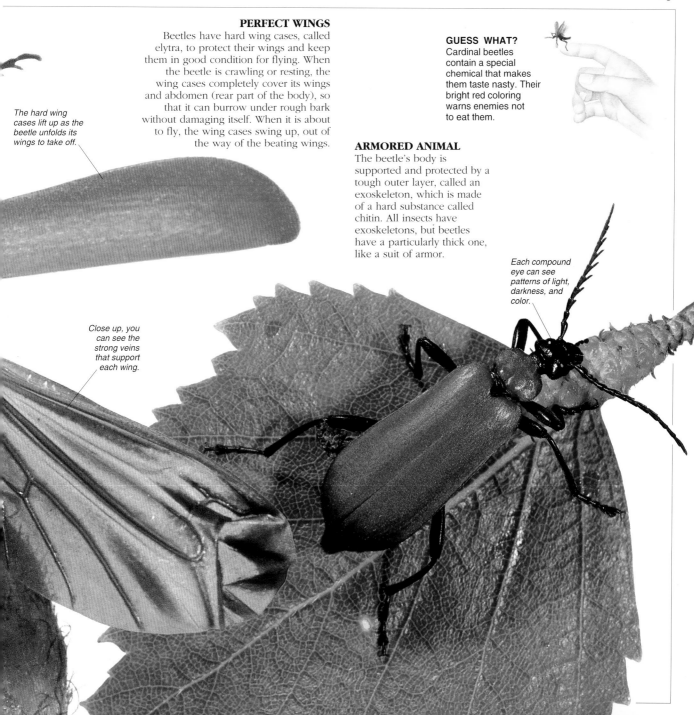

PERFECT WINGS
Beetles have hard wing cases, called elytra, to protect their wings and keep them in good condition for flying. When the beetle is crawling or resting, the wing cases completely cover its wings and abdomen (rear part of the body), so that it can burrow under rough bark without damaging itself. When it is about to fly, the wing cases swing up, out of the way of the beating wings.

GUESS WHAT?
Cardinal beetles contain a special chemical that makes them taste nasty. Their bright red coloring warns enemies not to eat them.

ARMORED ANIMAL
The beetle's body is supported and protected by a tough outer layer, called an exoskeleton, which is made of a hard substance called chitin. All insects have exoskeletons, but beetles have a particularly thick one, like a suit of armor.

The hard wing cases lift up as the beetle unfolds its wings to take off.

Each compound eye can see patterns of light, darkness, and color.

Close up, you can see the strong veins that support each wing.

FOREST FROGS

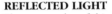

TREE FROGS LIVE IN dark, damp rain forests in the warmer parts of the world. The green skin of this Asian tree frog hides it from enemies, such as snakes, among the ferns and other plants covering the branches. Adults spend their time scrambling around up in the trees, searching for insects and other food. The female tree frog lays as many as 200 eggs on a branch overhanging a stream or pool, where the male fertilizes them. Then, using their back legs, they both beat the jelly surrounding the eggs into a froth. The froth dries and hardens on the outside, protecting the eggs until they hatch a week or so later. The tadpoles wriggle out and fall into the water, where they take about three months to develop into adult frogs.

GUESS WHAT?
Asian tree frogs, such as this one, often mate in one place, with many pairs adding to the mass of foam. There may be up to 3,000 eggs in one egg mass.

Special glands in the skin produce a slimy mucus, which keeps it moist.

The green skin helps disguise the frog among the leaves.

REFLECTED LIGHT
The green color of this frog is produced by special cells in the lower layer of the skin. These cells reflect light to produce a blue color. But, because of a yellow pigment (coloring) in the top layer of its skin, the frog looks green. Where there is no yellow pigment, the skin is blue.

The toes on the back feet are webbed.

The pupil closes to a slit to protect the eye in strong sunlight.

Bulging eyes allow the frog to see almost all the way around the head, so it can spot moving insects.

Frogs have good hearing but no external ears. Instead, the eardrum itself is on the outside of the head.

The mouth is wide and can hold a surprisingly large amount of food. It clamps down quickly on wriggling insects.

GRABBING A BITE

This frog waits patiently for dinner to come along. It is attracted by movement, and eats mostly insects, which it catches by flicking out its sticky tongue. But it will eat almost anything that is small enough to be crammed into its mouth. Tiny teeth in the roof of the mouth grip the victim, which the frog swallows whole.

These flat, moist pads cling on to wet leaves and slippery branches like suction pads.

Long legs allow the frog to jump and climb.

The fingers are only partly webbed, near the base.

COMMUNITY SPIRIT

THESE WOOD ANTS live in enormous groups, called colonies, in nests at the bases of conifer trees. The nests are built by wingless females, called worker ants. Above ground is a mound up to nine feet across, made of conifer needles, dry grass, and tiny twigs. Below ground is a maze of chambers and tunnels. The queen is usually the only adult female with wings, and the only female to lay eggs. She lays her eggs deep within the nest. Workers care for the young during the egg and larval stages, until they become young adults. Most of the eggs develop into workers, but some become males or new queens. On a warm, damp day in summer, swarms of young males and queens from all the nearby colonies fly high into the air to mate. The male ants die soon after mating, but the fertilized queens then start up new colonies.

Wood ants bite their enemies with these sharp mandibles (jaws), and squirt acid from their abdomen (rear part of the body) into the wound.

These compound eyes are made up of many tiny lenses that see a pattern of light and dark dots.

Joints allow the legs to bend, so the ant can climb and run.

The narrow waist makes the body very flexible.

FOOD FARMS

In the treetops, tiny aphids feed on a liquid called sap, which they suck from the leaves. The sap is partly digested by the aphids, then it oozes out of their rear ends as a sweet liquid called honeydew. Wood ants like to feed on honeydew, and they squeeze it out of aphids by stroking them with their antennae (feelers). Ants like honeydew so much that they carry about 600 pounds of it back to their nest every summer.

Claws help the ant grip on to surfaces when it is climbing.

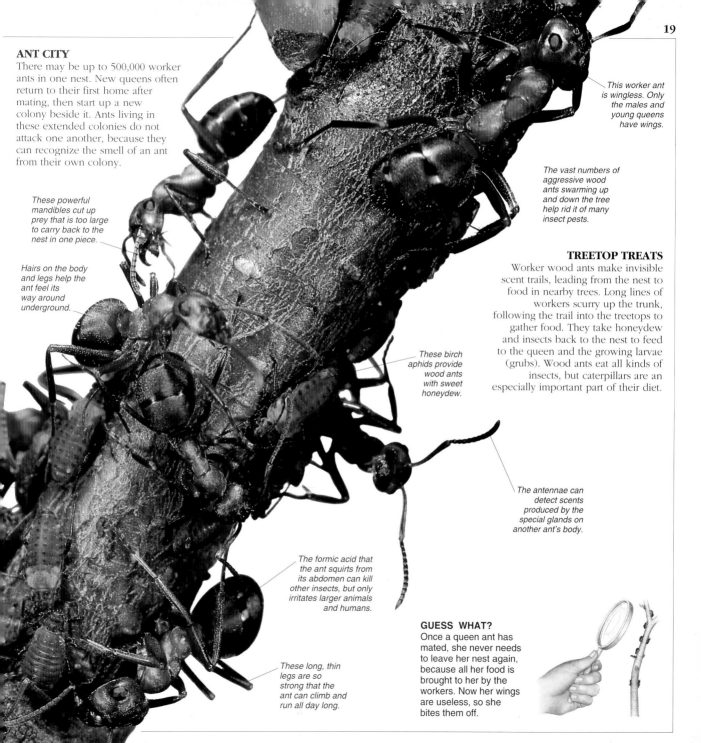

ANT CITY

There may be up to 500,000 worker ants in one nest. New queens often return to their first home after mating, then start up a new colony beside it. Ants living in these extended colonies do not attack one another, because they can recognize the smell of an ant from their own colony.

These powerful mandibles cut up prey that is too large to carry back to the nest in one piece.

Hairs on the body and legs help the ant feel its way around underground.

This worker ant is wingless. Only the males and young queens have wings.

The vast numbers of aggressive wood ants swarming up and down the tree help rid it of many insect pests.

TREETOP TREATS

Worker wood ants make invisible scent trails, leading from the nest to food in nearby trees. Long lines of workers scurry up the trunk, following the trail into the treetops to gather food. They take honeydew and insects back to the nest to feed to the queen and the growing larvae (grubs). Wood ants eat all kinds of insects, but caterpillars are an especially important part of their diet.

These birch aphids provide wood ants with sweet honeydew.

The antennae can detect scents produced by the special glands on another ant's body.

The formic acid that the ant squirts from its abdomen can kill other insects, but only irritates larger animals and humans.

These long, thin legs are so strong that the ant can climb and run all day long.

GUESS WHAT?

Once a queen ant has mated, she never needs to leave her nest again, because all her food is brought to her by the workers. Now her wings are useless, so she bites them off.

TRICK OR TREAT

THESE LARGE, JUICY puss moth caterpillars are tasty treats for birds. So in order to protect themselves from attack, they put on a threatening display that tricks birds into thinking the caterpillars are much larger than they really are. The puss moth caterpillar is the feeding and growing stage in the life cycle of a puss moth. In early autumn, it finds a suitable place on a tree trunk and prepares to pupate. The caterpillar makes a case, called a cocoon, with silk from a special organ called a spinneret. It mixes the silk with chewed-up fragments of bark. This disguises the case, to protect the insect during the winter. By spring, the caterpillar has completely changed shape, and has become a winged adult moth. It produces a chemical that softens the tough cocoon, then cuts its way out and flies off to begin its life in the air.

Red threads shoot out from these tails to scare off enemies.

FAST FOOD

On warm spring nights, adult puss moths fly around willow, sallow, and poplar trees, looking for a mate. The female moth lays up to three eggs at a time on the upper surface of the leaves. She usually lays them on more than one tree. This ensures that each caterpillar has enough food to eat without having to go far.

The sharp mandibles (jaws) are for cutting and chewing leaves.

These sharp barbs on the tails discourage enemies from eating the caterpillar.

KEEP YOUR DISTANCE

If an enemy approaches the puss moth caterpillar, a surprise is in store. The caterpillar suddenly draws its head back into its body, revealing a vivid red circle with two black spots that look like large eyes. At the same time, the two tails flick forward, and a fine red thread whips out from each. If this does not scare off the enemy, the caterpillar rears up and squirts out stinging formic acid from a special gland beneath its head.

Close up, you can see tiny holes, called spiracles, along the sides of the body. The caterpillar breathes through these holes.

TINY TOT

When the tiny larva first hatches, it is completely black with two little tails. Its tough, protective skin will not stretch, so in order to get bigger, the caterpillar grows a new skin underneath the old one, which it sheds. This is called molting. Caterpillars usually molt five or six times before they are fully grown.

GUESS WHAT?

This kind of moth is called a puss moth because the adult's body is covered in soft, silky hair, like a pussy willow.

These simple legs are for walking and holding on to twigs and leaves.

Rows of tiny hooks give a firm grip.

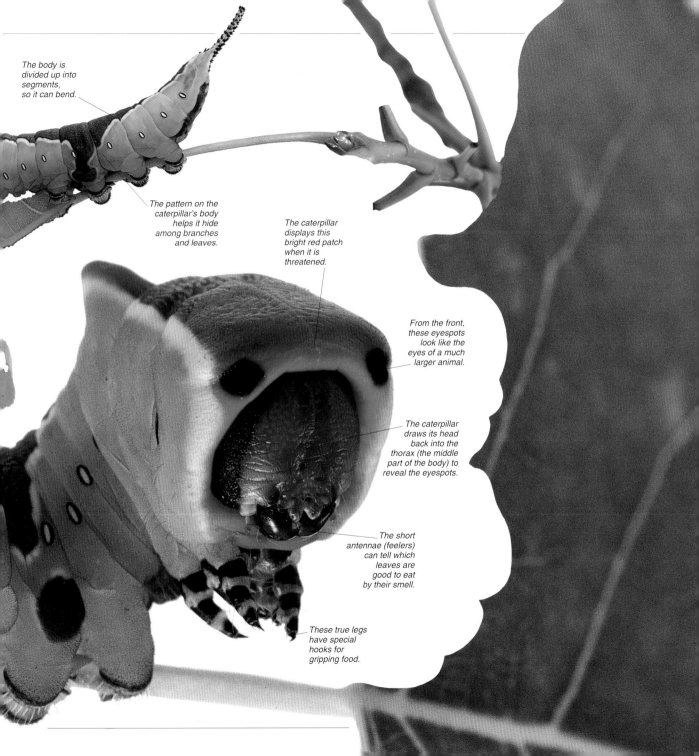

The body is divided up into segments, so it can bend.

The pattern on the caterpillar's body helps it hide among branches and leaves.

The caterpillar displays this bright red patch when it is threatened.

From the front, these eyespots look like the eyes of a much larger animal.

The caterpillar draws its head back into the thorax (the middle part of the body) to reveal the eyespots.

The short antennae (feelers) can tell which leaves are good to eat by their smell.

These true legs have special hooks for gripping food.

MINI MONKEY

HIGH UP IN THE CANOPY of the tropical rain forest, families of little marmosets scurry along the branches, twittering to each other in soft voices. Although marmosets are monkeys, they behave much like squirrels. They run and leap from branch to branch and sit nibbling fruits, which they hold in their front paws. Marmosets need to be very sure-footed in their treetop home, so they have sharp claws for gripping on to branches. They eat fruits and leaves, as well as small animals such as young birds, tree frogs, lizards, and insects. They are also fond of the sweet, gummy sap that oozes out of damaged trees. Sometimes they deliberately cut into a tree to make the sap flow. Marmosets are active during the daytime. At night, they hide away in tree holes, which give them shelter and protection.

Thick, well-groomed fur keeps the animal dry. The adults' fur is long enough for the young to cling on to for safety.

FAMILY MATTERS

There are usually between three and eight marmosets in a family group. There are two adult parents, and several youngsters. The adult males help care for their young, often carrying them around in the treetops.

GUESS WHAT?

Common marmosets are among the smallest monkeys in the world. Even the largest common marmosets weigh no more than a pound.

The marmoset grips food in its front paws.

All common marmosets have these ear tufts of long white fur.

LAPPING SAP
In order to make sap dribble out of a tree trunk, marmosets have to cut through the bark and into the living wood. They do this by biting into the tree with their top incisors (front teeth). Then they gnaw upward with their lower incisors and lap up the sweet juice.

Marmosets have very good eyesight. Their large eyes can spot food from a long distance.

The nostrils open out on each side of the flat nose.

GROOMING IN GROUPS
Members of a family group spend a lot of time every day grooming one another. Grooming is important for marmosets. As well as getting rid of parasites and tangles in their fur, it also acts as a form of communication. It helps them make friends with one another, and to decide which animals are the leaders of the group.

Sharp claws help the marmoset run and jump from branch to branch without falling off.

The striped tail is longer than the body, and helps the marmoset balance.

PERFECT PARENT

THROUGHOUT THE SUMMER, parent bugs are found on the leaves of birch trees, feeding on the juicy sap. Most other insects lay their eggs, then leave them to fend for themselves. But the female parent bug is a good mother, caring for her young and protecting them from enemies such as birds. That is why this kind of bug is called a parent bug. The female lays between 30 and 40 tiny eggs on the underside of a birch leaf. Then she stands guard over them, hiding them underneath her body, until they hatch two to three weeks later. Unlike many insects, which hatch as larvae (grubs), bugs hatch as miniature versions of the adults, but without wings. The young parent bugs, called nymphs, remain close together under their mother's body. Eventually, as the nymphs grow, they wander off to live by themselves. They molt (shed their skin) several times before they are full-grown adults with wings.

MINIATURE SHIELDS

A bug's exoskeleton (outer skin) is rigid, so it has to molt in order to grow. It sheds its skin several times before it is fully grown. After its final molt, the bug has wings. One group of bugs, including parent bugs, look just like shields when they fold their wings. That is why this group of bugs are also known as shield bugs.

GUESS WHAT?

You might think that a bug is a kind of beetle, but they are quite different. Bugs have two pairs of wings, whereas beetles only have one pair.

WINTER HIDEAWAY

Unlike many insects, parent bugs survive through the winter. They hide under flakes of bark and in wood cracks to avoid predators such as birds. When new birch leaves begin to open in the spring, the bugs come out again and start to feed.

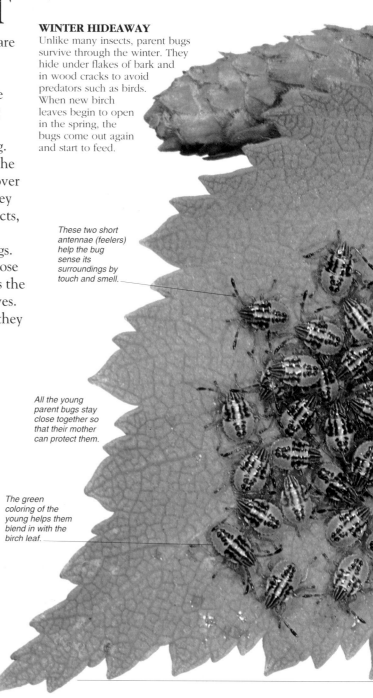

These two short antennae (feelers) help the bug sense its surroundings by touch and smell.

All the young parent bugs stay close together so that their mother can protect them.

The green coloring of the young helps them blend in with the birch leaf.

From above, it is easy to see why these bugs are also known as shield bugs.

This area of the forewing is hard. It protects the body underneath.

The compound eyes are made up of lots of individual lenses.

BEAKY BUG
The parent bug has long, narrow mouthparts, with four sharp cutters on the end. It uses these to pierce holes in leaves. Then it sucks up the sap using a tubelike mouthpart, called a rostrum, which is protected inside its beak.

Three pairs of short, jointed legs are attached to the middle part of the body, called the thorax.

The tip of the forewing is a clear membrane (a thin, transparent layer).

The tiny, brightly colored nymph looks similar to the adult, except that it has no wings.

LEAFY LIZARD

THIS MADAGASCAR DAY GECKO should be easy to spot. But, in fact, it is difficult to see, because it lives among the bright green leaves of the rain forest. As the name suggests, day geckos are active during the day. This is unusual, because most kinds of geckos come out only at night. Day geckos eat insects, fruit, and the sweet nectar from flowers. The female lays at least two clutches (batches) of eggs every year. There are only two eggs in each clutch. At first, the eggshells are sticky and soft. The gecko presses the eggs together and pushes them into a crack in tree bark. As the eggs dry, they harden and stick fast to the tree. The young hatch out after about nine weeks, breaking open their shells with a special egg tooth on the tip of the snout.

GUESS WHAT?
The gecko has a clever way of escaping from its enemies. If an attacker, such as a bird, grabs it by the tail, the gecko can run away and leave its tail behind. It grows a new one over the next few months.

SKIN FOR SUPPER
The scaly skin of a lizard cannot stretch as the lizard grows. So from time to time, when the skin gets too tight, the lizard sheds it, to reveal a new one which has grown underneath. This is called sloughing. To remove the old skin, the lizard rubs itself against rough surfaces. Then it pulls off the old skin with its mouth and eats it.

These large, round eyes give the gecko very good color vision.

After it has eaten, the gecko cleans its face and eyes with its long tongue.

This gecko cannot blink. Instead, each eye is protected by a transparent (clear) scale, called a brille.

Nostrils on the tip of the snout help the gecko find food.

These small, sharp teeth grip and crunch up food, such as insects.

ACROBATICS
Geckos are very agile. They can run along the undersides of branches upside down. Geckos can grip so well because they have tiny bristles on the undersides of their toes which can grasp even the tiniest bumps.

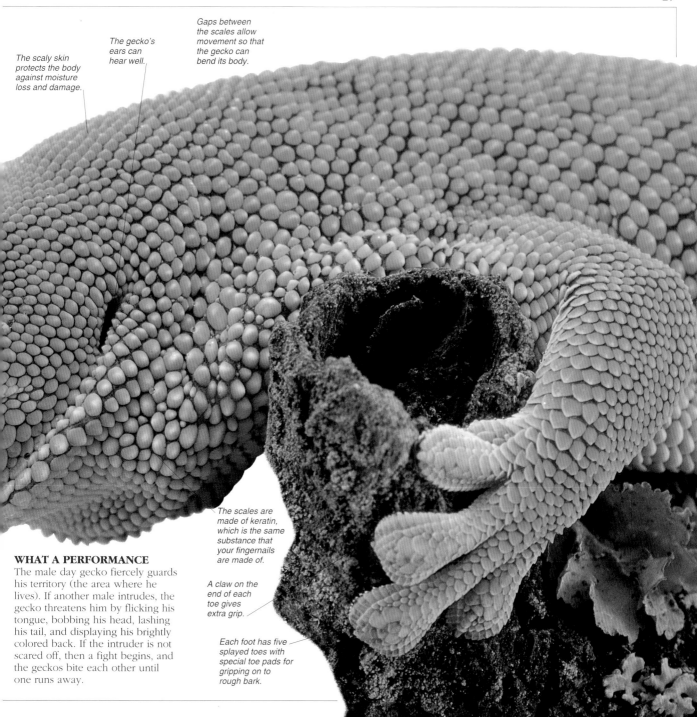

The scaly skin protects the body against moisture loss and damage.

The gecko's ears can hear well.

Gaps between the scales allow movement so that the gecko can bend its body.

The scales are made of keratin, which is the same substance that your fingernails are made of.

A claw on the end of each toe gives extra grip.

Each foot has five splayed toes with special toe pads for gripping on to rough bark.

WHAT A PERFORMANCE

The male day gecko fiercely guards his territory (the area where he lives). If another male intrudes, the gecko threatens him by flicking his tongue, bobbing his head, lashing his tail, and displaying his brightly colored back. If the intruder is not scared off, then a fight begins, and the geckos bite each other until one runs away.

These stout, sensitive antennae (feelers) can detect prey deep inside the gall.

The protective outer coat is called the cuticle. It is tough and watertight.

The chalcid wasp has two pairs of thin, transparent (clear) wings.

The long, thin antennae are for smelling, tasting, and touching.

The chalcid wasp uses its long ovipositor for laying eggs in the gall.

MARBLE MARVEL

IN SPRING AND SUMMER, female gall wasps lay their eggs inside the buds of oak trees. The wasp lays only one egg in each bud that she chooses. The egg hatches into a tiny larva (grub), which starts to eat the bud. As it feeds, it somehow causes the tree to make a marblelike gall in place of the bud. After four months they look like hard, brown marbles, measuring about 1 inch across. When the larva is fully grown, it turns into a pupa, enclosing itself in a pouch. Over the next two weeks or so, many changes happen to its body, until eventually an adult wasp climbs out of the pupa. Then it chews its way out of the gall, leaving a neat, round hole.

PARASITIC PERIL
A gall provides food and shelter for the developing larva inside. But the larva is not as safe as you might think. Parasites (animals and plants that live in or on another living thing) can find the larva inside its gall. The parasitic chalcid wasp bores a hole in the gall with its special egg-laying tube, called an ovipositor, and lays an egg inside. The chalcid wasp larva then hatches out and eats the gall wasp larva.

Male marble gall wasps are black and shiny.

A GALL STORY
Marble gall wasps that come out of the galls on English oak trees are always female. These females then lay their eggs in a different kind of oak tree, called a Turkey oak. Small, soft galls grow, and this time both male and female wasps come out. After the females from the Turkey oak have mated, they lay their eggs in English oak buds, and the complicated life cycle begins all over again.

The gall wasp's transparent wings are very delicate.

These chalcid wasp larvae have eaten the gall wasp larva that was growing inside this gall.

This adult chalcid wasp is burrowing its way out of the gall.

The center of the gall is nutritious.

The hard shell turns brown in the autumn.

The outside of the gall becomes woody.

GALL SORTS

There are many kinds of gall wasps, and each kind lays its eggs on a different part of a plant. Some lay them in the leaves, some in the roots, and others in the woody parts. Each kind of gall wasp has its own special gall. Some are small, and look like speckles on a leaf, but others, such as the gall of the oak apple gall wasp, are quite large, measuring up to 2 in. across.

GUESS WHAT?

The marble gall wasp gets its name from the galls in which the larvae develop. These are a similar size and shape to the glass marbles that you play with.

GLOSSARY

Abdomen *the rear part of the body*
Antennae *a pair of feelers*
Aphids *small insects that feed by sucking the sap from plants*
Colony *a group of animals or plants of the same kind that live together*
Compound eyes *eyes consisting of many separate lenses*
Exoskeleton *a tough covering on the body, made of a substance called chitin*
Larva *the young, grublike stage of an animal's life*
Metamorphosis *the transformation from a larva to an adult*
Molt *to shed the skin or exoskeleton*
Mucus *a slimy, often poisonous substance that certain animals produce*

Nymph *the larva of certain kinds of insects, such as dragonflies*
Parasite *a plant or animal that lives in or on another living thing*
Pollen *the dusty powder produced by many flowering plants for reproduction*
Proboscis *the long, strawlike mouthpart of an animal, such as a butterfly*
Pupa *the resting stage between a larva and an adult insect*
Sloughing *molting (snakes and lizards)*
Spiracles *the holes in an insect's exoskeleton through which it breathes*
Thorax *the middle part of the body, containing the heart and lungs*
Vibrations *tiny movements in air, in water, or underground*